W9-CBQ-063

"There is in this world no such force as the force of a man determined to rise. The human soul cannot be permanently chained."

— W. E. B. Du Bois

Corbis-Bettmann

W.E.B. Du Bois

By Don Troy

The Child's World®

GRAPHIC DESIGN
Robert E. Bonaker / Graphic Design & Consulting Co.

PROJECT COORDINATOR
James R. Rothaus / James R. Rothaus & Associates

EDITORIAL DIRECTION
Elizabeth Sirimarco

PHOTO RESEARCH
Ann Schwab / The Child's World, Inc.

COVER PHOTO
Portrait of W. E. B. Du Bois / Corbis-Bettmann

CURRICULUM COORDINATOR
Cynthia Klingel / Curriculum Director, School District #77, Mankato, MN

Text copyright © 1999 by The Child's World®, Inc.
All rights reserved. No part of this book may be reproduced
or utilized in any form or by any means without written
permission from the publisher.
Printed in the United States of America.

Library of Congress Cataloging-in-Publication Data
Troy, Don
W. E. B. Du Bois / by Don Troy.
p. cm.
Includes index.
Summary: A brief biography of the African American educator
and activist who helped found the NAACP and worked much
of his life to gain equitable treatment for his people.
ISBN 1-56766-555-1 (library reinforced : alk. paper)

1. Du Bois, W. E. B. (William Edward Burghardt),
1868-1963 — Juvenile literature. 2. Afro-Americans — United
States — Biography — Juvenile literature. 3. Civil rights workers
— United States — Biography — Juvenile literature. 4. National
Association for the Advancement of Colored People —Biography —
Juvenile literature.
[1. Du Bois, W. E. B. (William Edward Burghardt), 1868-1963. 2.
Civil rights workers. 3. Afro-Americans—Biography.] I. Title

E185.97.D73T76 1998   98-4328
305.896'073'0092 — dc21   CIP
[B]   AC

Contents

Born in the North

William Edward Burghardt Du Bois was born in Great Barrington, Massachusetts, on February 23, 1868. It was an important time in the nation's history because the American Civil War had ended only three years earlier. The entire country was undergoing tremendous changes.

The Civil War was a long, bitter fight between the nation's southern and northern states. It began when the South withdrew from the United States to form its own country. One reason the South left the Union was because northern leaders wanted to outlaw *slavery*.

Since the 1600s, many southerners had kept African slaves to work their fields, care for their homes, and do any other job asked of them — all without pay. Slaves were considered possessions, and White southerners bought and sold them like cattle. In 1865, the North won the Civil War, and slavery finally became illegal throughout the United States. The end of slavery, however, did not mean that *African Americans* had equal rights.

University of Massachusetts Archive

MARY SILVIA BURGHARDT DU BOIS AND WILLIAM, SHORTLY AFTER HIS BIRTH.

University of Massachusetts Archive

W. E. B. DU BOIS IN 1872.

University of Massachusetts Archive

WILLIAM'S FATHER ALFRED DIED WHILE HIS SON WAS STILL YOUNG, SO WILLIAM WAS RAISED BY HIS MOTHER AND AUNTS.

William's father died when his son was still a child. Although the Du Bois family was poor, William had a happy childhood, living with his mother and aunts. Smart, fast, and athletic, he was a leader among the boys in his small town. When he was old enough, William always had a part-time job to earn money for his family. Although the North was relatively *integrated* compared to southern states, William knew he did not always have the same opportunities as his White friends.

An excellent student, Du Bois graduated from high school with top grades. He had long dreamed of attending the country's oldest college, Harvard University, but his family simply could not afford to send him there. The minister of his church arranged for Du Bois to attend Fisk University instead.

Fisk University was a school for African Americans located in Tennessee, a southern state. William's family worried about sending him to the South, where there were strict *segregation* laws. Blacks and Whites were kept apart and treated differently. Nevertheless, William decided to take advantage of the opportunity to attend college. He packed his belongings and traveled to the South.

AFRICAN AMERICAN STUDENTS GATHER IN THE FISK UNIVERSITY CHAPEL FOR MORNING PRAYERS.

Library of Congress/Corbis

William studied hard, but he also devoted some of his free time to teaching African American children at nearby country schools. The people he met in these small southern communities were different from the families of Great Barrington.

William was saddened by the poverty and illiteracy that was so common among African Americans in the South. The segregation laws meant Blacks could not attend the superior White schools. Blacks were kept from the best jobs, and many couldn't find work at all. Although Black men had been granted the right to vote in 1870, Whites often threatened them if they attempted to cast their ballots. African Americans couldn't even eat in the same restaurants or use the same washrooms as Whites.

More disturbing were the stories of African Americans who were seriously mistreated. Sometimes racist Whites burned down the homes of Black families. Other times, they beat or even murdered them. At the time, *lynching* was a common practice in the South. When Blacks were murdered, no one was arrested or punished. Slavery was illegal, but African Americans still did not have basic *civil rights*.

William excelled in his college courses, but he learned more lessons than just those taught in the classroom. The more he discovered about the injustices African Americans suffered, the prouder he became of his own heritage. William believed that if African Americans could remain strong under even the most terrible conditions, they might one day achieve equality. He encouraged his classmates and other Blacks in the community to unite against *prejudice*. The rest of his life would be dedicated to exactly that cause.

Library of Congress/Corbis

A CROWD WATCHES AS WHITE MEN PREPARE A PLATFORM FOR THE LYNCHING OF AN AFRICAN AMERICAN MAN ACCUSED OF KILLING A WHITE GIRL. THE LYNCHING DREW A CROWD OF **10,000** PEOPLE IN THE SMALL TOWN OF PARIS, TEXAS, IN **1893**.

University of Massachusetts Archive

THE FISK UNIVERSITY GRADUATING CLASS OF 1888. WILL IS SEATED AT LEFT.

To Achieve Equality

In 1888, Du Bois graduated from Fisk with honors. His achievements were so impressive that Harvard University offered him a scholarship. In 1890, he graduated from Harvard with honors and a second college degree. Encouraged to learn more about the history of slavery and of his people, Du Bois decided to continue studying at Harvard.

During his years at Harvard, Du Bois developed his theory that *racism* was caused by ignorance. For many years to come, Du Bois would attempt to educate White Americans about Blacks. He intended to prove that Blacks were not inferior, as many Whites believed. Du Bois was convinced that if the United States offered all of its people equal rights and a good education, the result would be increased success for the entire nation.

In 1895, Du Bois completed his studies, becoming the first African American to receive an advanced degree (called a Ph.D.) from Harvard. He was one of the most highly educated Americans of his day, but no White university would hire him. He finally found a job teaching Latin and Greek at Wilberforce, a small university for African Americans in Ohio. At Wilberforce, Du Bois would meet and marry his first wife, a student named Nina Gomer.

Du Bois took the job at Wilberforce because he had to earn a living, but he did not plan to spend his life teaching. He wanted to do much more with his education, and he wanted to dedicate himself to achieving a better life for African Americans.

Du Bois returned to the South in 1897 with Nina to teach history at Atlanta University in Georgia. The university asked him to conduct research about African Americans. Du Bois believed this was the chance he had hoped for and planned to prove through scientific research that Blacks were not inferior. He wrote 16 books about his findings.

Du Bois' studies showed that like people everywhere, African Americans were shaped by their history, their living conditions, and their education. Given equal opportunities, they learned as quickly and could achieve as much as their White counterparts.

Scholars around the world welcomed and accepted his findings. He gave speeches and wrote articles that presented Blacks and Whites as equal human beings. Unfortunately, his efforts had little effect on the world around him.

Segregation and racism did not go away. His books were on the shelves of public libraries, but southern libraries wouldn't let him inside the door because of his skin color. Du Bois was invited to speak before members of Congress, but he couldn't ride in a Whites-only train to get there.

In 1903, Du Bois wrote a book of essays called *The Souls of Black Folk*. It stressed that the most serious problem in 20th-century America was the separation of Whites and Blacks. Du Bois became the voice of protest against segregation and racism in the United States.

Joseph Schwartz Collection/Corbis

THE SOUTH'S SEGREGATION LAWS WERE INTENDED TO KEEP AFRICAN AMERICANS SEPARATE FROM WHITE PEOPLE.

University of Massachusetts Amherst

THE FACULTY OF ATLANTA UNIVERSITY POSES FOR A PHOTOGRAPH IN 1906. DU BOIS (STANDING IN THE BACK ROW, SECOND FROM THE RIGHT) TAUGHT AT THE UNIVERSITY FROM 1897 THROUGH 1910.

Library of Congress

In 1881, Booker T. Washington founded the Tuskegee Institute, a school for African Americans, in Alabama.

One of the essays in his book criticized Booker T. Washington, an African American leader who was respected by both Blacks and Whites. Washington felt it was more important that African Americans have food, shelter, and good jobs than equality or integration. He believed equality would come naturally if Blacks proved themselves to be intelligent and hardworking.

In a famous 1895 speech in Atlanta, Washington told African Americans to accept segregation — for the time being — in exchange for education and jobs.

He was convinced that over time, African Americans would earn respect. This speech later became known as the Atlanta Compromise: Washington suggested that Blacks compromise by accepting less than they truly wanted.

Washington was the founder of the Tuskegee Institute, a school that trained Blacks to help them find jobs. The students learned skills such as cooking and blacksmithing, but they did not have an opportunity to study history, languages, or science.

THE TUSKEGEE INSTITUTE WAS BUILT BY ITS STUDENTS IN 1885. SINCE 1985, IT HAS BEEN KNOWN AS TUSKEGEE UNIVERSITY.

AP Wide World

Du Bois thought Black students deserved more. "We want our children trained as intelligent human beings should be," he said, "and we will fight for all time against any proposal to educate Black boys and girls simply as servants and underlings, or simply for the use of other peoples. They have a right to know, to think, to aspire."

As time went on, Washington was disappointed to see that Blacks were not being treated any differently. He remained patient, but Du Bois was convinced that a new approach was necessary. He felt that Washington's acceptance of segregation might have seemed like the right thing to do at one time, but this was no longer the case. Du Bois believed that African Americans must demand equal treatment, and he encouraged people to protest and take action.

In 1905, Du Bois organized the Niagara Movement, a meeting of African American businesspeople, teachers, and ministers held at Niagara Falls in Canada. The organization primarily dedicated itself to attacking Washington's ideas. The Niagara Movement met until it fell apart in 1909 — in part because of opposition from Booker T. Washington.

University of Massachusetts Amherst

DU BOIS (SEATED IN FRONT) AND THREE OTHER MEMBERS OF THE NIAGARA MOVEMENT IN 1906. THE ORGANIZATION DEDICATED ITSELF TO PROTESTING THE MISTREATMENT OF BLACK AMERICANS.

University of Massachusetts Amherst

MEMBERS OF THE NIAGARA MOVEMENT AT THE 1906 MEETING IN HARPER'S FERRY, WEST VIRGINIA. THE GROUP MET FOUR TIMES UNTIL THE MEMBERS DISBANDED IN 1909.

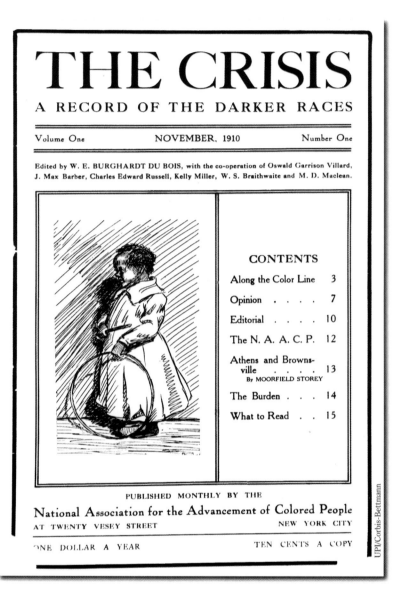

THE FIRST ISSUE OF *THE CRISIS,* THE NAACP'S MONTHLY MAGAZINE, WAS PUBLISHED IN NOVEMBER 1910. DU BOIS EDITED THE PUBLICATION UNTIL 1934.

A National Association

The battle between Washington and Du Bois continued, but Washington had strong supporters with a lot of money, many of whom were White. They considered Du Bois a troublemaker and began to pressure Atlanta University leaders to fire him, threatening to withdraw financial support if they did not. By 1910, the university gave in, and Du Bois was out of a job.

In 1910, the members of the Niagara Movement united once again, joined by other groups, to form the National Association for the Advancement of Colored People. (At that time, African Americans were often called "colored people.") The organization was best known by its initials, the NAACP. This new organization would play a powerful role in the battle for Black civil rights throughout the 20th century.

Du Bois became the NAACP's director of publications and research. He moved to Harlem, New York, and for the next 25 years edited the NAACP magazine, *The Crisis.*

Dedicated to the fight against segregation and racism, *The Crisis* staff investigated the ongoing mistreatment of Blacks. Du Bois learned, for example, that African American soldiers were being mistreated on French battlefields during World War I. When the war ended, Du Bois went to Europe to investigate and was shocked by what he learned.

He published a French government document titled "Secret Information Concerning Black American Troops" in *The Crisis*. The document told French officers how to treat African American soldiers:

"The black man is regarded as an inferior being. . . . We must prevent the rise of any pronounced degree of intimacy between French officers and black officers. . . . We must not commend too highly the black American troops, particularly in the presence of white Americans. . . . Make a point of keeping the native population from spoiling these negroes. "

The Crisis sold 125,000 copies of the issue before the government directed the United States Post Office to stop delivering it. Government agents came to the NAACP offices looking for the troublemakers who published it. When the agents asked Du Bois what his organization was fighting for, Du Bois answered, "We are fighting for the enforcement of the Constitution of the United States." *The Crisis* had become one of the most important African American magazines in the country.

The National Archives/Corbis

AFRICAN AMERICAN SOLDIERS RETURN TO THE UNITED STATES FROM FRANCE IN 1919. *THE CRISIS* INVESTIGATED THE MISTREATMENT OF BLACKS IN THE MILITARY DURING WORLD WAR I.

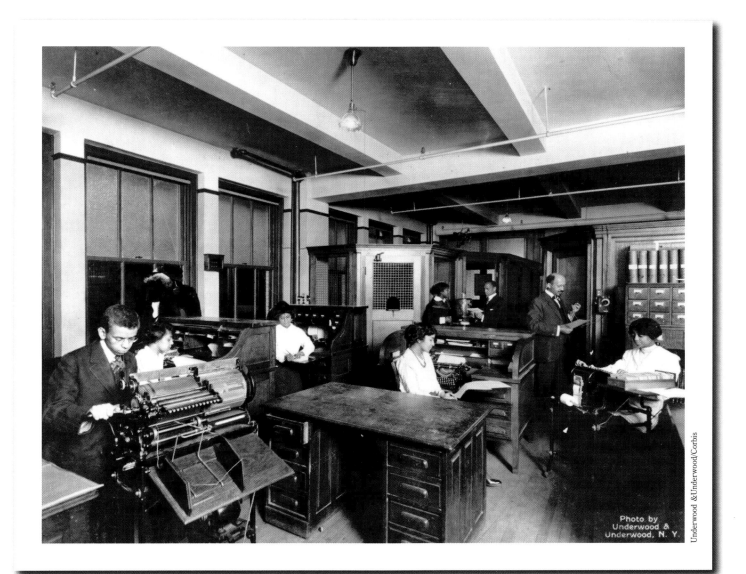

Underwood &Underwood/Corbis

DU BOIS (STANDING AT RIGHT) REVIEWS AN ARTICLE AT THE OFFICE OF *THE CRISIS*. AFRICAN AMERICAN WRITERS, EDITORS, AND ARTISTS WORKED HARD TO PUBLISH THE MONTHLY MAGAZINE, ONE OF THE FIRST DEDICATED TO CIVIL RIGHTS.

African American artists drew the covers for *The Crisis*, and African American authors wrote its poems, stories, and news articles. Du Bois' "Men of the Month" section featured prominent African Americans. "With this monthly magazine," Du Bois once said, "I could discuss the Negro problem and tell White people and colored people just what the NAACP was and what it proposed to do."

During his years at the NAACP, Du Bois also began to promote *Pan-Africanism*, the belief that all people of African descent have a common background and should cooperate with one another. He encouraged Blacks across the African continent, and in the United States and other nations, to consider themselves as one people, striving to achieve equality and justice wherever they lived. Between 1919 and 1926, with the NAACP's support, he helped organize four Pan-African conferences with attendees from around the world.

Over time, Du Bois began to have difficulties with other leaders at the NAACP. For one thing, he wanted complete control of the content of *The Crisis*, but others at the NAACP would not give up their say. Then, during the 1930s, millions of Americans, Black and White, found themselves unemployed during the Great Depression. In Harlem, where Du Bois lived, people were evicted from their homes and went hungry.

Du Bois felt that if African Americans were to survive, they needed a new plan. He proposed they band together and form *cooperatives* in which African Americans would start their own factories, farms, and businesses, separate from White communities. Blacks would do the work, and Blacks would share the profits.

Du Bois published this idea in *The Crisis*, and other NAACP leaders disagreed with him. The NAACP promoted integration, but Du Bois' ideas were another form of segregation. Du Bois resigned from the NAACP in 1933.

UPI/Corbis-Bettmann

THE GREAT DEPRESSION LEFT MILLIONS OF AMERICANS WITHOUT JOBS IN THE 1930s. BREAD LINES WERE ESTABLISHED TO FEED THOSE WHO DID NOT HAVE ENOUGH MONEY TO BUY FOOD FOR THEMSELVES AND THEIR FAMILIES.

A Decade of Writing

Du Bois was 66 years old when he left *The Crisis,* an age when many people retire. He chose instead to return to Atlanta University. During the 10 years that followed, he wrote a number of his most important works.

In 1935, Du Bois wrote a book titled *Black Reconstruction*, exposing untrue information that had been published about African Americans by White writers and historians.

Many prejudiced historians claimed the freed slaves were ignorant and dishonest, arguing that freedom was dangerous for these "inferior beings." They claimed the *Reconstruction*, a difficult period in southern history, was made all the more so by "lazy" freed slaves who refused to work and generally caused trouble for White people. Such views, written by respected southern scholars, were used to enforce segregation laws.

Du Bois exposed these untruths in his book, *Black Reconstruction*. He described the vital contributions of African Americans during the South's recovery and explained that within five years of the war's end, the cotton crop was fully restored. In the next five years, crops were stronger than ever. The South's economy, Du Bois argued, recovered quickly — even without the free labor the slaves had provided.

In 1939, Du Bois started *Phylon,* a magazine dedicated to Black race and culture issues. In 1940, he published *Dusk of Dawn*, an autobiography. Then he published the introduction to an encyclopedia about Blacks for which he served as editor-in-chief.

University of Massachusetts Amherst

DU BOIS LEFT HIS POSITION AT *THE CRISIS* IN **1933**, BUT HE CONTINUED TO DEDICATE HIMSELF TO THE WRITTEN WORD IN THE DECADES THAT FOLLOWED.

AP Side World Photos

IN 1944, NEAR THE END OF WORLD WAR II, DU BOIS ATTENDED THE CONGRESS OF PARTISANS OF PEACE, WHICH WAS HELD IN PARIS. THE ATTENDEES DISCUSSED WORLDWIDE EFFORTS TO END THE WAR AND PREVENT OTHERS IN THE FUTURE.

In 1944, Du Bois faced another troubling example of racism in his own life. His outspoken criticism of segregation and prejudice offended many southerners. Atlanta University's wealthy supporters threatened to withdraw financial assistance if Du Bois remained on the faculty. NAACP leaders heard of his dismissal and invited him to return to the organization as the director of research. They encouraged him to devote his time and effort to race issues in foreign lands.

Before leaving Atlanta University, Du Bois had written two books about the African continent, *Color and Democracy* and *The World in Africa*. For most of his career, Du Bois had protested against the existence of European colonies in Africa. Across the continent, European nations had used military power to take over huge expanses of land. Much of northern Africa, for example, was part of the French West Africa colony, while England colonized much of eastern Africa.

In 1945, Du Bois called for a new Pan-African Congress in England. The meeting was a success, and important Black leaders from nations around the world attended. In fact, three African attendees later became the first prime ministers of Ghana, Kenya, and Nigeria when those nations won independence in the following decades.

Library of Congress/Corbis

THE HEADQUARTERS OF THE NAACP IN NEW YORK CITY. DU BOIS RETURNED TO WORK FOR THE NAACP IN 1944.

An African Ending

In the early 1950s, Du Bois thought about the 60 years he had spent fighting racism. He saw little progress. The United States was a democracy and should therefore offer all its citizens equal rights. Black Americans, however, continued to be discriminated against nearly 200 years after the Constitution was written.

For many years, Du Bois had been studying the ideals of *communism*, a form of government that attempts to make all people equal. Ideally, no one in a communist society is richer than anyone else, and no one is judged by skin color. Communist leaders seriously discourage the practice of religion as well, believing religion causes disagreements between people with differing views.

In the 1950s, the United States was in the middle of the "Cold War" with communist nations. Communism challenged the ideals on which the United States Constitution was based, so anticommunist feelings were strong.

Corbis/Bettmann

DURING THE 1950s, SENATOR JOSEPH McCARTHY (CENTER) ACCUSED MORE THAN 200 AMERICANS OF COMMUNIST ACTIVITIES.

Corbis-Bettmann

Du Bois with his second wife, playwright and biographer Shirley Graham. The two were married in 1951. His first wife Nina died in 1949.

Library of Congress/Corbis

DU BOIS WAS FREQUENTLY CALLED UPON TO TESTIFY ON BEHALF OF BLACKS, BOTH IN THE UNITED STATES AND AROUND THE WORLD. HERE HE TESTIFIES BEFORE THE U.S. SENATE REGARDING THE ONGOING MISTREATMENT OF BLACK AFRICANS LIVING IN EUROPEAN COLONIAL SETTLEMENTS.

Du Bois began to speak publicly about communism. In 1951, one week before his 83rd birthday, he was arrested, charged with being a communist spy. There was no evidence to support the charges, so he was found not guilty. His reputation, however, was badly damaged. Publishers would not accept what he wrote, and no one invited him to speak anymore.

Although the United States tried to forget Du Bois, the newly independent African nations did not. African leaders called him for advice. The president of Ghana, Kwame Nkrumah, invited him to his country. Calling Du Bois "friend and father," Nkrumah asked him to work on the *Encyclopedia Africana*. Du Bois, now 90 years old, accepted the invitation.

In 1963, Du Bois proudly became a citizen of Ghana. He said: "My great grandfather was carried away in chains from the Gulf of Guinea. I have returned that my dust shall mingle with the dust of my forefathers."

That same year, William Edward Burghardt Du Bois died in Ghana on August 27th. An honor guard carried his flag-draped coffin to the shore where he would be buried, a spot less than 100 yards from where many Africans had been shipped to America and then forced into slavery. Often called the Father of Pan-Africanism, Du Bois died a citizen of a young African nation, a nation that could thank him for his commitment to freedom and equality for Blacks around the world.

PRESIDENT KWAME NKRUMAH OF GHANA, AFRICA, IN 1961.

Hulton-Deutsch Collection/Corbis

In the United States, one day after his death, a civil rights march was held in Washington, D.C. One speaker at the event was a new African American leader, Dr. Martin Luther King, Jr., a man 60 years younger than Du Bois.

"One idea [Du Bois] insistently taught," King once said, "was that Black people have been kept in oppression and deprivation by a poisonous fog of lies that depicted them as inferior . . . .

Du Bois recognized that the keystone in the arch of oppression was the myth of inferiority, and he dedicated his brilliant talent to demolish it."

King studied and respected the works of Du Bois and recognized his contributions to the civil rights cause. Without Du Bois' lifelong effort, the 1963 civil rights march — and all the steps taken toward true equality for African Americans — might never have happened.

Wide World Photos/Globe Photos

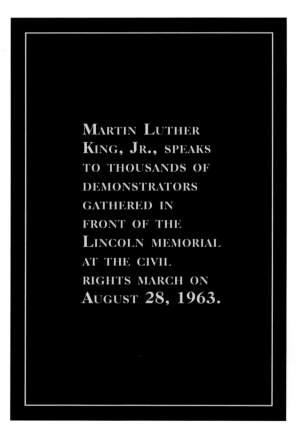

MARTIN LUTHER KING, JR., SPEAKS TO THOUSANDS OF DEMONSTRATORS GATHERED IN FRONT OF THE LINCOLN MEMORIAL AT THE CIVIL RIGHTS MARCH ON AUGUST 28, 1963.

The National Archives/Corbis

PROTESTERS HOLD UP SIGNS DEMANDING CIVIL RIGHTS FOR AFRICAN AMERICANS AT THE FAMOUS DEMONSTRATION THAT TOOK PLACE THE DAY AFTER W. E. B. DU BOIS' DEATH.

Corbis-Bettmann

Timeline

1865	The American Civil War ends. African American slaves are freed.
1868	William Edward Burghardt Du Bois is born in Great Barrington, Massachusetts.
1888	Du Bois graduates with honors from Fisk University.
1890	Du Bois graduates from Harvard University with honors and a second university degree.
1895	Du Bois is the first African American to earn a Ph.D. from Harvard University. He accepts a teaching position at Wilberforce University in Ohio.
1903	Du Bois' book, *The Souls of Black Folk,* is published.
1905 to 1909	The Niagara Movement meets to organize and protest against the segregation of African Americans.
1910	The National Association for the Advancement of Colored People (NAACP) is formed. Du Bois is the editor of the organization's magazine, *The Crisis*.
1919 to 1926	Du Bois helps organize Pan-African congresses, encouraging people of African descent to unite. One goal of the organization is to end European control of Africa.
1933	Because of disputes with other members, Du Bois resigns from the NAACP and his position at *The Crisis*. He returns to Atlanta University to write and teach.
1944	Du Bois returns to the NAACP as its director of research.
1945	Du Bois calls for a new Pan-African Congress in England.
1951	Du Bois is arrested under suspicion of being a communist spy. Shirley Graham and Du Bois are married.
1958	Du Bois accepts Premier Kwame Nkrumah's invitation to come to Ghana.
1963	Du Bois becomes a citizen of Ghana. He dies later that year in his new country.

Glossary

African Americans
Americans whose ancestors came from the African continent. In the past, African Americans were called colored people and Negroes.

civil rights
The rights guaranteed to all American citizens by the Constitution and its amendments.

communism
A system of government that believes in eliminating personal property so that all goods are common property. Other differences, such as religious beliefs, are also eliminated to equalize members of society.

cooperatives
An organization that combines the efforts of many people united to work toward a common goal.

integrated
A society or institution that does not separate people according to race, class, religious beliefs, or ethnic group is said to be integrated.

lynching
A murder that is carried out by a mob of people; at least 3,000 African Americans were lynched by White gangs between 1880 and 1970 in the southern United States.

Pan-Africanism
A movement encouraging all people of African descent, regardless of where they live, to cooperate with one another and act as a single group. The prefix "pan" means to involve or unite all.

prejudice
A bad feeling or opinion about something or someone without just reason; feeling anger toward a group or its characteristics.

Reconstruction
The period in the South after the American Civil War in which the seceded states had to rebuild.

racism
The belief that one race is naturally superior to another.

segregation
The separation or isolation of a race, class, or ethnic group.

slavery
The practice of forcing a person or group of people to work for others without pay.

Index

For Further Information

Hine, Darlene Clark, Hauser, Pierre N., and King, Martin Luther (editor). *Great Ambitions from the "Separate but Equal" Doctrine to the Birth of the NAACP.* Broomall, PA: Chelsea House Publishers, 1995.

Senna, Carl. *The Black Press and the Struggle for Civil Rights.* Danbury, CT: Franklin Watts, 1994.

Stafford, Mark. *W. E. B. Du Bois (Black Americans of Achievement).* Broomall, PA: Chelsea House Publishers, 1991.

Weber, Michael. *The African American Civil Rights Movement (Causes and Consequences).* Austin, TX: Raintree/Steck Vaughn, 1998.

The following Web sites offer more information about W. E. B. Du Bois:
http://www.duboislc.com
http://members.tripod.com/~DuBois/index.htm

About the Author

Don Troy was born and raised in Boston, Massachusetts. He received his Ph.D. from Boston University in 1971, and was certified as a Total Family Therapist by Boston Family Institute in 1973.

He taught at Stonehill College in Massachusetts from 1963 to 1973. Moving to California in 1973, he spent four years as director of a national trade association for marriage and family educators and counselors.